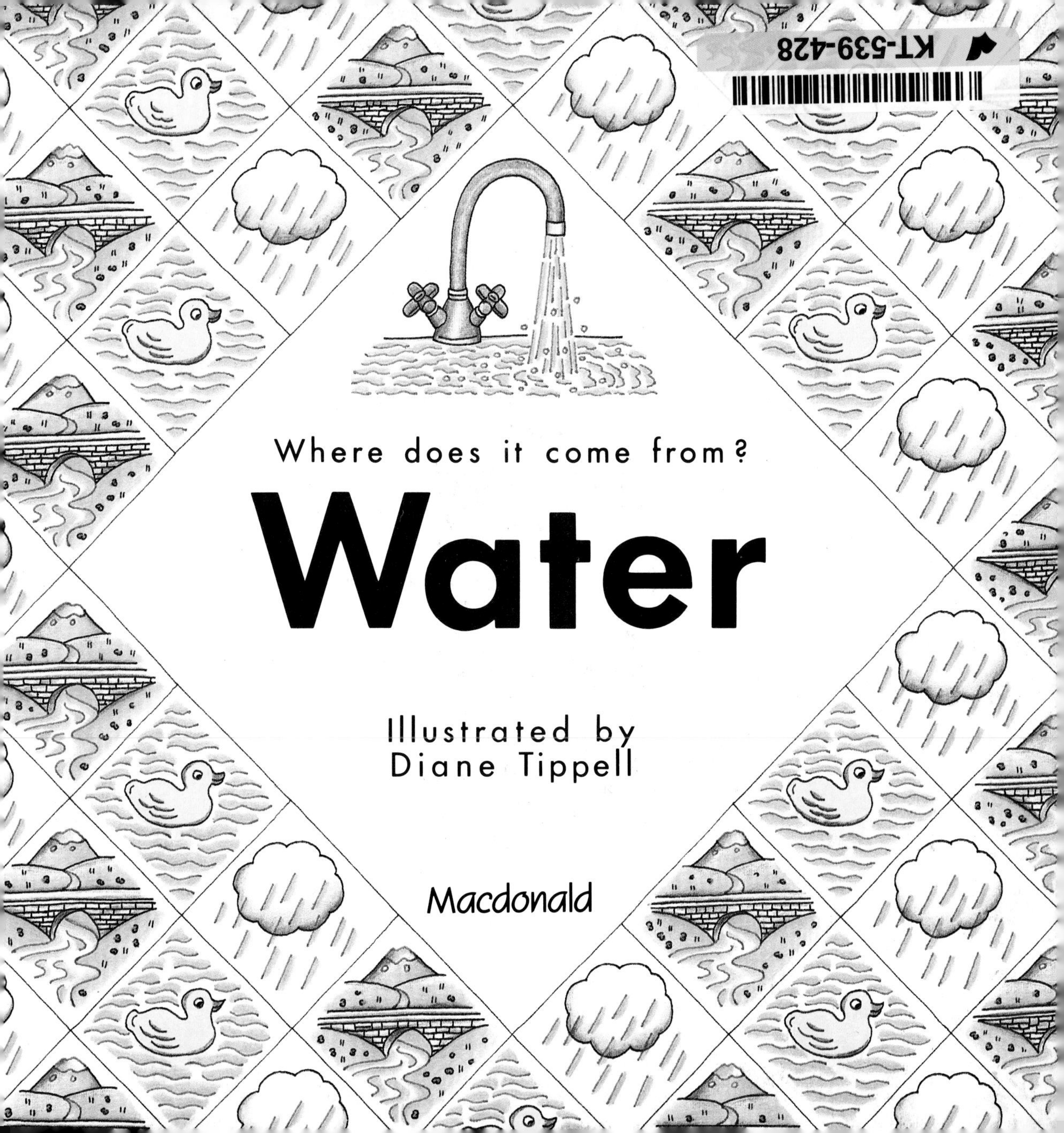

Where does it come from?

Water

Illustrated by
Diane Tippell

Macdonald

There's water everywhere here. It bubbles up from under the ground at the spring where the children play. It dribbles down the mountains as the snow melts. More water falls as rain.

At first the water runs down the fields in trickles. The trickles join to make little streams. The streams get bigger as they flow and join up to become small rivers.

It's raining here too but where does the water go? It bounces on the roads and cars and people and houses. It runs down the roofs and drainpipes to the ground. It gathers in the gutters, picking up dirt and rubbish as it goes. And it splashes down the drains into big underground sewer pipes which carry it away.

The sewer pipes bring the town's dirty water to the sewage works to be cleaned. Some of it has come from the streets but most comes from inside the houses, from sinks and baths and lavatories.

Big bits of rubbish, like rags and tin cans, are taken out in the screening house. Other dirt is taken out as sludge in the tanks you can see. In the end the water is clean enough to join all the other water from the hills and the fields in the river.

The river has come a long way, getting bigger and bigger all the time. Now a dam is blocking the way and the water has spread out to make an artificial lake. This is the reservoir. Water is stored here until it is needed. Meanwhile it gets used for other things. Can you see what?

The reservoir water is not pure enough to drink. So big pipes take it into the waterworks to be cleaned. Here the water runs through filter beds filled with gravel and sand which catch tiny bits of dirt like a sieve.

The filter beds have to be kept clean too. Can you see the machine taking the dirty sand out?

Now the water has chemicals added to it to keep it pure as it sets out on its journey through the pipes to our homes.

From now on the water travels through pipes to keep it clean. They are buried underground so they are out of the way. Sometimes the water has to travel up hills to get to where it is needed. So along the way there are pumping stations like this one, full of powerful pumps to push it along. The people at the pumping station decide which pipes the water travels along. When one place has got enough water for the moment they can switch it off and send it to a different place.

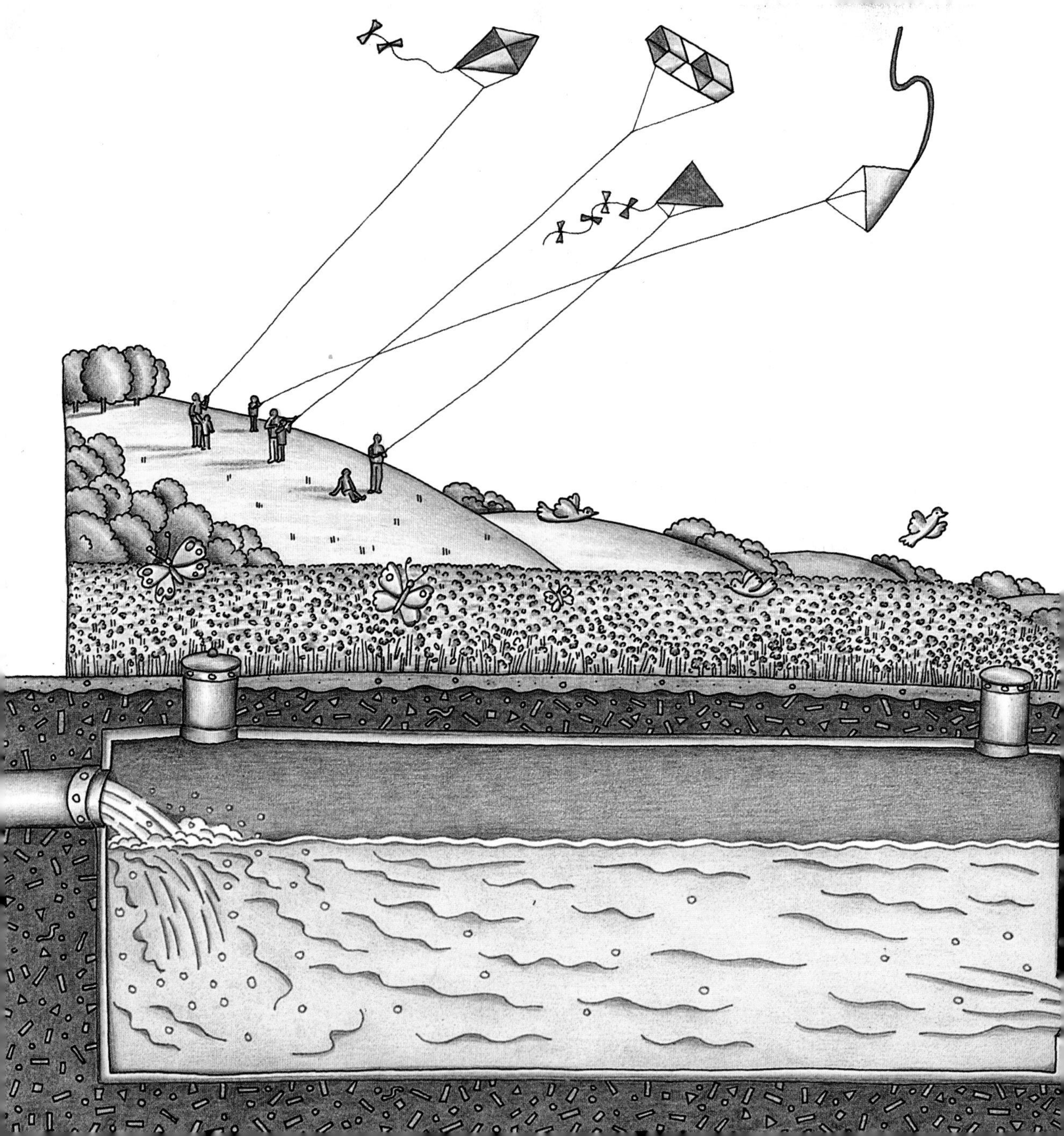

Before it gets to our houses the pure water is pumped to large service reservoirs. These have to be on high ground so the water can flow downhill to the houses, shops and factories when people need it. If the ground isn't high enough the water is pumped up into tall water towers instead.

Early in the morning when everyone is getting up, washing, cleaning their teeth and having a drink, lots of water is used and the water in the reservoir gets very low. At other times, like the middle of the night when not many people are using water, it has time to fill up for the next day.

Oh dear. There seem to be problems here!
On its way to the houses and shops the water runs through more pipes buried under the road. Most of the time you would never know they were there at all. But sometimes one cracks and starts to leak. The men from the waterboard are digging a hole in the road to fix it. And over there, the firemen have fixed their hosepipes to a special tap, called a fire hydrant.

Each house has its own pipe carrying water from the big pipe under the road. There's a tap just outside the house to turn the water off if something needs to be mended. Inside the house more small pipes carry the water along under the floors and behind the walls to the washing machine, the kitchen sink and up to the hot water tank, the bath, the shower and the lavatory.